Trade Liberalization in
Aviation Services

AEI STUDIES ON SERVICES TRADE NEGOTIATIONS
Claude Barfield, series editor

THE DOHA ROUND AND FINANCIAL SERVICES NEGOTIATIONS
Sydney J. Key

INSURANCE IN THE GENERAL AGREEMENT ON TRADE IN SERVICES
Harold D. Skipper Jr.

LIBERALIZING GLOBAL TRADE IN ENERGY SERVICES
Peter C. Evans

REDUCING THE BARRIERS TO INTERNATIONAL
TRADE IN ACCOUNTING SERVICES
Lawrence J. White

TRADE LIBERALIZATION IN AVIATION SERVICES:
CAN THE DOHA ROUND FREE FLIGHT?
Brian Hindley

Trade Liberalization in Aviation Services

Can the Doha Round Free Flight?

Brian Hindley

The AEI Press

Publisher for the American Enterprise Institute

WASHINGTON, D.C.

2004

Available in the United States from the AEI Press, c/o Client Distribution Services, 193 Edwards Drive, Jackson, TN 38301. To order, call toll free: 1-800-343-4499. Distributed outside the United States by arrangement with Eurospan, 3 Henrietta Street, London WC2E 8LU, England.

Library of Congress Cataloging-in-Publication Data

Hindley, Brian,
    Trade liberalization in aviation services : can the Doha Round free flight? / Brian Hindley.
        p. cm.
    Includes bibliographical references.
    ISBN 0-8447-7171-6 (pbk.)
    1. Aeronautics, Commercial—Freight—Deregulation. 2. Trade regulation. 3. Free trade. I. Title.

HE9788.H56 2004
387.7'4—dc 22

                                            2003063555

1 3 5 7 9 10 8 6 4 2

Printed in the United States of America

Contents

Foreword

In advanced industrial economies, the service sector accounts for a large portion of each nation's gross domestic product. Despite the increasing importance of services trade, the multilateral trading system began establishing rules to open markets in those sectors only in 1995, with the creation of the General Agreement on Trade in Services (GATS) at the conclusion of the Uruguay Round of trade negotiations. Decisions at the end of the round did provide for continuing negotiations in the services area. Only with the renewed commitment to a new round of trade negotiations, undertaken in November 2001 at the World Trade Organization (WTO) ministerial meetings in Doha, Qatar, however, did serious individual sectoral negotiations go into high gear.

The American Enterprise Institute is engaged in a research project to focus on the latest round of trade negotiations on services. The project, mounted in conjunction with the Kennedy School of Government at Harvard, the Brookings Institution, and the U.S. Coalition of Service Industries, entails detailed analyses of individual economic sectors: financial services, accounting, insurance, energy—and now the air transport sector. The series will conclude shortly with a study of audiovisual and entertainment services. Each study identifies major barriers to trade liberalization in the sector under scrutiny and assesses policy options for trade negotiators and interested private-sector executives.

AEI would like to acknowledge the following donors for their generous support of the trade-in-services project: American Express Company, American International Group (AIG), CIGNA Corporation, FedEx Corporation, Mastercard International, the Motion

Picture Association of America, and the Mark Twain Institute. I emphasize, however, that the conclusions and recommendations of the individual studies are solely those of the authors.

In this monograph, Brian Hindley analyzes the implications of the application of GATS disciplines to air transport services (including airline passenger, air cargo, and express-delivery services), as well as the alternative of forming a transcontinental aviation area (TCAA) outside of the GATS. In contrast to other services areas, at the establishment of the GATS in 1995, air transport services were excluded; thus, WTO members remain free to create a stand-alone TCAA agreement.

In chapter 2, Hindley describes the unique characteristics of the air transport industry that present particular problems and issues for trade liberalization. He notes that a fully liberalized international air transport system would not only allow carriers from country A to own and provide flights between countries B and C, but also allow flights within any of the three countries (and to other outside markets). Because of political and economic realities, such an idealized system today is impossible to achieve. The study describes three national restrictions that present obstacles to liberalization: cabotage restrictions, ownership restrictions, and wet-leasing restrictions. Cabotage occurs when a country B carrier takes passengers or cargo from one point in country A to another point in country A. Governments typically prohibit such activity. The United States and a number of other WTO members maintain restrictions on foreign holding in domestic airlines. Wet leasing is a practice whereby a carrier pays another company to provide it with aircraft or crews to fly under the carrier's own colors. The study also analyzes—and rebuts—the argument that nationality rules for air transport ownership are necessary for national security reasons.

The next section of the monograph addresses what Hindley calls the "airport problem." This problem involves issues related to locational services such as the provision of utilities, transportation to, from, and within the facility, and telephone and other telecommunications services. The most difficult questions, however, revolve around "slots"—the access of carriers to gates and runways at a particular airport at a particular time. Hindley analyzes in detail the competitive tradeoffs that flow from government ownership or regulation of a privatized system of allocating slots. He concludes:

> Ownership and control of airports is a central issue in the liberalization of international civil aviation. Liberalization of the latter almost certainly cannot proceed without reform of the former. Reform is not straightforward from a political point of view. In particular, incumbent carriers are likely to oppose it. . . . Nevertheless, it does not make much sense to talk about liberalization of international air transport without acknowledging the need to cut the Gordian knot of airport ownership and control.

Chapters 4 and 5 of the book represent the core analysis of the negotiating options for air transport services. Chapter 4 discusses the potential—and the pitfalls—of pursuing liberalization within the GATS; and chapter 5 describes an alternative scenario of focusing on express-delivery services, separate from other air transport services. On the topic of the GATS and air transport services, Hindley points out that with regard to two fundamental principles of the WTO— most-favored-nation (MFN) obligations and national treatment— special circumstances prevail for air transport services. In the first place, air traffic rights (routes, slots, etc.) in relation to air transport services are explicitly exempted from GATS disciplines. With this as a backdrop, the study explores the possibility of concluding bilateral or plurilateral agreements that would not necessarily include all WTO members. Hindley posits that such agreements would be feasible under the GATS as presently constituted because of the general exemption from MFN obligations.

Similarly, with regard to national treatment (equal treatment of domestic and foreign carriers within national borders), though there is no explicit exemption, GATS rules in this area are not strong. According to Hindley, the rules would not necessarily prohibit such practices as restrictions on foreign investment, cabotage, wet leasing, and various slot allocation schemes.

The fly in the ointment is dispute settlement within the WTO. It is Hindley's view that, while there might be negotiated substance compromises on a number of issues, key areas would have to be settled through dispute settlement, where WTO panels and the WTO Appellate Body would have the final word—with no recourse to veto by industry or governments. He concludes:

> Dispute settlement . . . raises difficulties that may prove to be insuperable. On the one hand, there is no possibility of air transport services entering the GATS without becoming subject to WTO dispute-settlement procedures, even if only in the final stages of a dispute. On the other hand, there is little prospect that the U.S. air transport industry will willingly accept the supremacy of the WTO in this regard.

A final negotiating option, explored in chapter 5, is to separate a portion of the air transport industry—express-delivery services—and bring these services into the GATS first, leaving negotiations on other segments of the industry for later. Express-delivery services are an important and growing component of the total air transport industry. It is estimated that they earn over $45 billion annually and employ more than 400,000 people worldwide. Hindley argues that a number of countries are aware of the benefits of liberalization of express-delivery services, just as they had been earlier with regard to telecommunications services, where special rules had been negotiated in the GATS. This might tip the balance toward liberalization in the current round of trade talks.

Several short-term goals have been advocated by express-delivery companies. First, reforms are needed to address the inefficient and inconsistent customs procedures that afflict express-delivery mail and packages. Trade facilitation through standardization of customs procedures has substantial support, even among developing countries, and thus is a top candidate for early results. More difficult issues arise from competition between express-delivery providers and national post offices. The study analyzes—and rebuts—arguments in favor of retaining public monopolies in postal services, but it also sets forth principles for competition between the public monopolies and private sector providers. The GATS has already dealt with these issues in the area of telecommunications services, and Hindley suggests that, as with telecommunications, a special *Reference Paper* explicitly laying down rules for competition might be negotiated for express-delivery services. Such a paper would include, among other elements, safeguards against cross-subsidization, rules for provision of universal service, and licensing criteria for the private delivery of express-delivery services. Hindley concludes:

> Undoubtedly . . . the greatest hopes for the outcome of the Doha Round as far as aviation or aviation-intensive industries are concerned lie with express delivery. . . . [Such an agreement would] deal with, or encompass, the difficulties facing express delivery—on customs procedures, nontariff barriers to delivery of the service, and the issues raised by competition with public postal operators. Supporters of the GATS should enthusiastically press for that route to be followed.

CLAUDE BARFIELD
American Enterprise Institute
for Public Policy Research

1

Introduction

International Air Transport and the General Agreement on Trade in Services

In one of his last acts as Director-General of the World Trade Organization (WTO), Mike Moore appealed to governments to apply WTO rules to international air transport (Moore 2002). International air transport, he said, is exempt from the General Agreement on Trade in Services (GATS):[1]

> The result has been a myriad of centrally planned arrangements, of either a bilateral or plurilateral nature, which have ensured that competition has been stunted, customer service eroded and that the poorest countries have once again been given short shrift. (Moore 2002)

These centrally planned arrangements arise because international civil air transport is still organized on a foundation of bilateral agreements between states, as agreed in Chicago in 1944—not a banner year for liberal trade policy. "Today," Moore continued,

> there are some 3000 bilateral deals between countries which determine the access airlines have to foreign markets. . . . There are vast restrictions on foreign ownership, on route capacity and on cabotage—the right for foreign carriers to fly between two points in the same country. (Moore 2002)

Moore's comments are elaborated upon in the following pages. Little elaboration is needed, however, to see that for an industry in the state described by Moore, a case for liberalization might be made.

For air transport, however, the GATS, as advocated by Moore, is not the only route to liberalization. Because air transport is currently exempt from the rules of the GATS, arrangements that are closed to other industries are open to it. The United States, the European Union (EU), and other interested parties are, for example, legally free to form a transcontinental aviation area (TCAA)—a free trade area for aviation only. Such an arrangement could, in principle, liberalize aviation within the TCAA without reference to the WTO, and without the difficulties created by the requirement that proposals before the WTO obtain the assent of all of its members.[2]

In fact, negotiations on a TCAA are currently in progress between the United States and the European Commission. The idea of such an arrangement certainly interests some carriers and some governments.

Some carriers, though, especially in the United States, prefer the status quo and support continuing negotiation by the United States of "open-skies" agreements. Open-skies agreements are certainly an improvement on the rigid old-style bilaterals, which specified in minute detail flight frequencies, capacity, airports of departure and arrival, and prices. These bilaterals still reign in much of the world, where there are few hints of a liberal impulse in policy toward air transport.

But while open-skies agreements abandon this detailed regulation, they are still government-to-government bilateral agreements. They prevent the entry into international routes of carriers other than the limited number designated in the agreement. Why does air transport, alone among today's industries, need such a foundation? Whatever answer the industry offers to that question, the existence of alternatives increases the difficulty of winning acceptance of the GATS by carriers.

Nor is this the only disability of the GATS. The collapse of the WTO ministerial meeting in Cancun in September 2003 cast a shadow over the future of the WTO itself, and therefore over the future of the GATS. Most likely, however, the Doha Round will be revived; though probably not until after the U.S. presidential elections in 2004. Even if the United States and the EU arrive at an agreement on a TCAA, relations between the TCAA and the rest of the world will need regulation and adjudication of disputes. The GATS is an obvious vehicle for achieving those goals. Other structures may eventually be judged better for these roles; but it would be irresponsible not to *consider* the GATS.

A full analysis of the economic costs and benefits of the GATS, of course, would include more than the views of carriers. In particular, it would embrace the interests of *users* of air transport services and might very well arrive at conclusions that carriers would find uncongenial. It is a simple political fact, though, that the lack of enthusiasm of major carriers for the GATS hampers efforts to win broader application of the GATS to the air transport industry, however parochial the economic basis for that lack of enthusiasm.

Conversation and correspondence suggest, however, that members of the air transport industry are occasionally misinformed about the GATS, sometimes seriously so. Supporters of the GATS, on the other hand, sometimes lack knowledge of the industry and the ways in which the GATS might have to be modified to take account of its characteristics.

This study therefore sets out the implications of a broader application of the GATS to air transport. The appendix provides some basic statistical information about the industry. Chapters 2 and 3 identify those aspects of it that invite liberalizing efforts. Chapter 4 analyzes the issues raised by an attempt to apply the GATS to air transport as a whole. Chapter 5 assesses the potential for beneficial application of GATS principles to air freight, where indications are that liberalization might be less strongly opposed than in passenger services. It is difficult to separate the two sectors, since much freight is carried on aircraft that also carry passengers, and this creates technical difficulties for efforts to liberalize freight without similar measures for passenger traffic. The chapter continues, however, with an examination of express air cargo services—an aviation-intensive sector that has shown a strong interest in the GATS and may offer greater possibilities for its application in the immediate future than air transport in general or air freight in general. Conclusions to the analysis are presented in chapter 6.

2

Liberalization and
Barriers to Liberalization

Industries that provide services often possess unique features, and useful thought about liberalizing the provision of a service must take these singular characteristics into account.

International air transport is a good example. One way of focusing on the characteristics of the air transport industry that are relevant to liberalization is to ask what "liberalization" of international air transport might mean.

Scope of Liberalization

"International air transport" must, at a minimum, include flights between countries A and B by carriers of those countries. In a minimally liberal system, any A or B carrier could legally serve any route between A and B, as long as the carrier met the safety and other legitimate requirements of the governments of A and B.

International civil aviation as currently organized fails to meet this minimal condition. Even open-skies agreements are based on "designated carriers"—carriers *not* designated in the agreement may not fly the routes between A and B.

A fully liberalized global aviation system, however, would go further. Routes between countries A and B would be legally open to carriers from countries C, D, and E, subject, of course, to meeting the safety and other legitimate requirements of A and B.

A further step is logically possible. If carriers from countries A, B, and C are allowed to offer services *between* A and B, why not on routes *within* those countries?

That situation, it might be objected, is not international. But it is, albeit in a different sense than with flights between countries. An Italian architect residing in Italy, for instance, who designs a house for an American citizen residing in the United States, with the house to be placed on a site in the United States, is engaged in an international transaction in services. An Italian carrier transporting American citizens within the United States would similarly be engaged in an international transaction.

Even at this early stage, the importance in these propositions of the national qualifier—an *Italian* carrier or a *U.S.* carrier—should be noted. In other industries, such terminology verges on the anachronistic. A subsidiary in the United States of a Japanese or German automobile manufacturer, for example, is regarded, certainly for most legal purposes, as a U.S. company, subject to U.S. laws and regulations.

If this were true in civil aviation, and a country C carrier could easily establish and own, or acquire, an A or B carrier, a fully liberalized system would follow from the freedom of any A or B carrier to fly routes between A and B. If an A carrier can easily become, establish and own, or acquire a B carrier, then the freedom of B carriers to fly routes within country B implies that country A carriers will also have easy access to those routes.

In fact, civil aviation is so far from any of these states of affairs that to mention such arrangements, which clearly are *logically* possible, is to risk being branded by aviation specialists as, at best, extremely impractical. Perhaps the specialists are right—practicality is an issue to be explored later on. Nevertheless, it is worth noting that genuine liberalization of international civil aviation must mean for the world a state of affairs akin to the one that exists within the United States today, in which a U.S. carrier is legally free to enter any domestic U.S. route.

U.S. carriers are regulated for safety purposes, and this is perfectly compatible with genuine liberalization (although regulation, even for safety purposes, can raise problems in an international context when different jurisdictions apply different regulations). When regulations differ among countries, moreover, they can be used for protective purposes—to favor carriers of one nationality over carriers of another. The central point in the present context, however, is that liberalization does not imply that safety regulation must be abandoned or weakened.

Regardless of the safety status of a potential foreign entrant, internal U.S. routes, for example, are reserved for U.S. carriers. A European or Asian carrier might be willing to offer seats between New York and Los Angeles at half the price of the cheapest U.S. carrier, and U.S. passengers might happily accept that offer. U.S. law, however, does not permit the offer to be made. The United States prohibits cabotage—the transport of passengers or freight on internal U.S. routes by non-U.S. carriers. Only U.S. carriers can legally operate on internal U.S. routes. Moreover, being a "U.S. carrier" is not simply a matter of registering a company in the United States and buying some airplanes. A carrier cannot be a "U.S. airline" if foreigners hold more than 25 percent of its voting shares.

Obstacles to Liberalization

Whatever the form of liberalization—whether a bilateral agreement, an agreement involving several countries, or a full-blown multilateral liberalization in the GATS—a number of basic problems and issues must be faced. In this chapter, several of these are discussed. One very important issue, however—the allocation of space and facilities at airports—is reserved for the next chapter.

Nationality Restrictions on Commercial Operations. Restrictions on commercial operations based on nationality take three primary forms:

- Cabotage restrictions: Cabotage occurs when a country B carrier picks up passengers or cargo at one point in country A and takes them or it to another point in country A. Typically, the government of A prohibits such movements; usually, only country A carriers are allowed to offer services between points in A. Nothing in the legal structure of international air transport, however, requires such a prohibition, and there are exceptions: Australia, for example, has recently permitted cabotage between its major cities.

- Ownership restrictions: The United States is not alone in maintaining restrictions on foreign holdings in "U.S. airlines." Many countries have similar restrictions. Canada and New Zealand have limits on foreign ownership similar to those of the United States. Australia allows 49 percent foreign ownership (though an airline flying only domestic Australian routes can be 100 percent owned by foreigners). A "European Union (EU) airline" must be majority-owned by EU citizens.

  Other countries have no such regulations. In some (for example, Argentina), foreigners can own a majority share in a (or the) national carrier. In rather more countries, however, the issue never arises; the national carrier is owned by the national government, and the government has no interest in selling.

- Wet-leasing restrictions: Wet leasing is a practice whereby a carrier pays another company to provide it with an aircraft and crew to fly under the carrier's own colors. The U.S. government does not allow U.S. carriers to wet-lease from lessors outside of the United States.

Interactions. Restrictions on cabotage, ownership, and wet leasing interact with one another. In the context of liberalization, the relationship and interaction between the restriction on cabotage and that on foreign ownership are probably the most important. Together, these restrictions prevent foreign carriers from offering services in domestic markets. Removal of either one would alter that situation. But removal of the prohibition on cabotage would have a different effect than removal of that on foreign ownership.

The essential difference lies in the regulations that apply to a foreign provider of services. If cabotage is permitted, foreign providers are subject to the regulations of their own countries.[3] A foreign-owned domestic company, on the other hand, is subject to domestic regulations. If both cabotage and foreign ownership are permitted, foreign carriers can choose the legal basis for their supply of services—that is, they can choose which set of regulations applies to their operations.

Opposition to cabotage often centers on wages. If the United States, for example, allowed unrestricted cabotage, foreign carriers using crews from low-wage countries could compete in the U.S. market. Employment of U.S. workers in the U.S. air transport industry, and/or their wages, might well be forced downwards. That U.S. labor unions oppose the granting of cabotage rights to foreign carriers is not surprising.

To allow foreign carriers to establish U.S. subsidiaries, however, would have a quite different effect. The U.S. subsidiary of a foreign carrier would be subject to the same U.S. laws and regulations that apply to carriers owned by U.S. citizens. In particular, the foreign-owned subsidiary would be obliged to hire crews from the same pool as U.S.-owned carriers—the pool made up of persons legally able to work in the United States

Why U.S. labor unions should oppose this state of affairs is much harder to understand. A foreign-owned carrier might be tougher with its labor force and the unions representing it than U.S.-owned carriers, though that seems unlikely—U.S. employers do not have the reputation of being softer in such matters than employers elsewhere. A foreign-owned carrier might try legal maneuvers that U.S. carriers have not tried, though that also seems unlikely, and, since both would be subject to the same U.S. laws, the maneuver must be open to U.S. carriers. Greater competition among airlines in the U.S. market might make it harder for unions to extract wage increases, though if competition reduced the price of transport, it would also probably increase travel and, with it, employment in the air transport industry.

Safety is another concern. Foreign carriers, it is said, could evade U.S. safety regulations, using aircraft that U.S. airlines are not permitted to use. But while cabotage does not intrinsically require application of the safety regulations of the country in which the service is supplied, that country can require such application as a condition of allowing cabotage. And if the United States allowed foreign ownership, U.S. safety regulations would fully apply to foreign-owned carriers established in the United States

Finally, this discussion of the first two types of restriction helps to clarify the position of the third: wet leasing. Were U.S. carriers permitted to wet-lease without restriction, they would be in a position to use low-wage foreign crews on internal U.S. services. A likely effect would be to reduce the demand for high-wage U.S. crews.

Trade in Goods and Trade in Services

Discussion of the relaxation of a regulation in terms of one interest only, though, is misleading. Allowing the purchase of U.S.-owned carriers by foreigners probably would benefit those U.S. owners; widening the market for the shares of their companies is unlikely to harm their share prices. The introduction into the domestic market of more competition is likely to benefit users of air transport.

In this context, though, "competition" has problematic features. The free flow of *goods* between countries means that low-wage foreign workers compete with high-wage U.S. workers. Low-wage foreign workers may compete so effectively—as they do in the garment industry, for example—that U.S. firms cannot survive without public support, which is typically provided by means of tariffs and/or quantitative restrictions on the competitive imports. U.S. officials nevertheless often profess support for free trade.

Were cabotage permitted, U.S. crews paid U.S. wages would compete with foreign crews paid foreign wages, which might be much lower than U.S. wages. How, though, in principle, does this competition differ from that found in international trade? Why should the one be advocated but the other rejected?

One difference is, of course, the location of the competing foreign workers. In standard international trade, they are located in their own countries. In cabotage, they are present in the United States itself. But while this might raise questions about immigration law, it does not seem to affect the validity of the underlying analytical principle. If competition between low-wage and high-wage workers by means of flow of goods is economically desirable, why is competition by means of rival offers of services in the domestic market undesirable?

The question comes close to the heart of a major issue in the liberalization of trade in services. Trade in goods typically takes place by manufacturing an automobile, say, in one location and shipping it to another. Neither producer nor purchaser has to change location for this to occur.

Delivery of many services, on the other hand, requires the provider of the service to be in the same location as the thing or person receiving it. This does not *necessarily* mean the provider has to be where the receiver is, but that is often the case. Air transport is an illustration. Trips from New York City to Kansas City could, in principle, be open to international competition. But a French carrier cannot manufacture trips from New York City to Kansas City in France and ship them to America; to offer trips from New York City to Kansas City, it has to have aircraft and crews operating in the United States. To prohibit it from doing so is to ban its participation in that trade, and is the service trade equivalent of a prohibitive tariff.

Alliances

The effect of such prohibitions is to prevent arrangements that both passengers and carriers might find advantageous. A European carrier, for example, might prefer to maintain a U.S. hub—with a high frequency of flights from its European home base and connecting flights to other North American destinations—rather than scheduling flights from its home base direct to a large number of U.S. cities. U.S. law, however, does not allow that.

Alliances between carriers provide a means of ameliorating that difficulty, and they have spread throughout the industry. Table 3 of the Appendix lists the principal alliances as they stood at the end of 2001. In principle, alliances can operate almost as one airline, offering passengers one-stop ticket purchases, coordinated arrival and departure scheduling without changing terminals, and reciprocal access to the airport lounges and frequent flyer benefits of the alliance partners. Critics, however, question whether these purported benefits are delivered in practice.

Even if an alliance does achieve in practice what it offers in principle, it is obviously possible that the benefits would be better delivered by a single airline, able, with its subsidiaries, to operate wherever in the world it wished. It is sometimes suggested that alliances remove the need to think about restrictions based on nationality. That alliances ameliorate the problems created by the restrictions is true. If the restrictions have no valid basis in the first place, though, why settle for amelioration?

The Defense Dimension

An important concern that stands apart from the economic issues discussed so far is defense. Aircraft that transport civilian passengers and cargo can also transport military passengers and cargo. From the standpoint of a military planner, the fleet of civil aircraft is a pool to be drawn upon in case of national emergency. The existence of such a pool allows the standing fleet of military transport aircraft to be smaller than would otherwise be possible, allowing defense resources to be allocated to other uses.

In the United States, the Department of Defense (DOD) represents this interest. Under its Civil Reserve Air Fleet (CRAF) program, U.S. carriers pledge to provide aircraft for military use when called upon to do so. In exchange, the U.S. Air Mobility Command (AMC) awards peacetime airlift contracts to civilian carriers that offer aircraft to the CRAF, which includes all major U.S. carriers. The CRAF website[4] says that the largest such contract is the international airlift services contract. In fiscal year 1999, the guaranteed portion of this contract was $345 million, but the AMC estimated that it would also award more than $362 million in additional business. Contracts under the "Fly America" program, under which U.S. government employees on business fly only on the aircraft of designated U.S. airlines, are also open only to CRAF participants. Only U.S.-owned carriers are eligible for the CRAF.

The principle that civil aircraft should be available for military use in case of national emergency is accepted here. There is still a question, though, of whether the principle justifies DOD opposition to changes in the nationality rules for ownership of U.S. carriers, cabotage, and wet leasing.

The DOD seems to believe that its military concerns require the United States to have the largest possible fleet of U.S.-owned civil aircraft. It supports the nationality rules discussed above as a means of achieving that end. In the view of some well-informed observers, DOD opposition is the primary obstacle to changing those rules.

DOD reluctance to rely on aircraft that are foreign owned, based abroad, and operating outside the United States is easy to understand. Whether such aircraft would in fact be available to the U.S. military in an emergency, even if they were contracted to be available, must be in doubt. It is easy to think of emergencies in which foreign governments opposed to a U.S. position or action might press their nationals to resist the transfer of aircraft to U.S. military use. Even in the absence of action by a foreign government, owners of aircraft based outside the United States are likely to find it easier to evade the transfer of their aircraft to U.S. military use than the owners of U.S.-based aircraft.

These facts, however, do not make a compelling case for opposing a right of establishment in the United States for foreign-owned carriers. Foreign-owned carriers operating in the United States as U.S.-incorporated entities would seem at first sight to be in the same position as U.S.-owned carriers. They would be subject to the same laws and penalties, and the crews of their aircraft would be American citizens (or other persons authorized to work in the United States).

The sole difference is the nationality of owners. That suggests that DOD opposition to a right of establishment is based on a belief that it will be easier in time of emergency for the DOD to obtain aircraft from U.S.-based carriers owned by U.S. citizens than from U.S.-based carriers owned by foreign nationals. That belief might be based on the notion that penalties for nonperformance can more easily be imposed on U.S. citizens. But while this argument might be plausible with regard to foreign-owned and foreign-established carriers, it is hard to see why it should apply to U.S.-established, foreign-owned carriers.

The weakness of the argument that it would be more difficult to penalize foreign owners of U.S.-based carriers suggests that DOD opposition might rest on a different basis: the patriotism of U.S. owners. The belief that patriotism will facilitate the transfer of aircraft to military use in an emergency may be correct. Another, no doubt more cynical, view would be that no owner—U.S. or foreign—will enthusiastically give up an aircraft for military use if there are valuable alternative uses for it. It is certainly desirable from a DOD standpoint that the penalty for breaking a CRAF contract should exceed the cost of fulfilling it, regardless of the nationality of the contractor.

Even if the DOD regards patriotic impulses as central to the success of the CRAF, though, nothing prevents the United States from giving a right of establishment to foreign-owned carriers while restricting membership of the CRAF to U.S.-owned carriers, as currently defined.[5] The DOD, however, is likely to object that opening internal routes to foreign competition might reduce the total fleet of U.S.-owned carriers. Such a development, it would probably say, would reduce the capacity of U.S. carriers to enter CRAF commitments.

It is possible that a right of establishment for foreign-owned carriers in the United States might reduce the size of the U.S.-owned fleet of civil aircraft, even though U.S. carriers presumably would gain similar rights in other countries. It is also possible to imagine a world in which CRAF contracts cannot be enforced without the spur of patriotism, even with respect to aircraft based in the United States. That either of these conditions would hold in the real world, however, seems unlikely. The DOD's concerns about the availability of aircraft in national emergencies are proper, but they do not seem to justify blocking the liberalization of international air transport.

All of the above takes the CRAF on its own terms. What would happen if, as some observers have suggested, the DOD were to rely on the market for the lease of aircraft and crews to obtain civil aircraft in an emergency? One problem with that approach is that the DOD might need aircraft with special specifications—the transportation of military equipment might require extra wide doors, for example, or reinforced floors. Under the CRAF program, such specifications can be accommodated. But insofar as such requirements are military and have few advantages for civilian use, a private market will not provide appropriate aircraft.

Could the DOD use the market in a reverse direction—that is, buy the aircraft it needs and lease them under contracts that require their immediate return in the event of a national emergency? It is said that the DOD dislikes this idea because it would require the purchase of aircraft to be a budget item, whereas the call on aircraft under the CRAF does not require expenditure on aircraft to be shown—although, of course, payments associated with the CRAF are exactly that.

If that is all there is to the DOD preference for the CRAF over purchasing and leasing its own aircraft, it must be said that it displays a monumental lack of seriousness. To block the liberalization of international air transport to preserve U.S. military capabilities is one thing. To do so in order to preserve a convenient method of accounting is quite another.

State Aid

State aid to some carriers presents a threat to unsubsidized carriers. Unsubsidized carriers, understandably, resist the idea of being forced into competition with subsidized carriers. They oppose a liberalization that might have that result.

Carriers are often owned by governments, which may use that position to provide disguised subsidies to them. Even if they do not wholly own "national" carriers, governments often subsidize their operation. Presumably this is done for reasons of national prestige.

From the standpoint of competing unsubsidized carriers, though, the rationale behind subsidies does not matter. From their perspective, subsidies unfairly tilt the playing field against them.

Agreement by unsubsidized carriers from country A to the liberalization of services between A and B, therefore, is likely to require assurances that the government of B will not subsidize B carriers. While reasonable, this requirement will likely present a major barrier to liberalization if the B government does not believe that B airlines are competitive with those of A, but is unwilling to allow them to go out of business.

A distinction should be drawn, however, between a situation in which subsidies to B carriers from the B government threaten the existence of A carriers, and one in which subsidies are necessary for B carriers to survive, but still allow A carriers to prosper. In the latter case, some agreement may be possible regarding the amount of subsidy that is allowable, and the circumstances in which it may be paid. It may be possible, in other words, to draw a line between aggressive subsidization and defensive subsidization, and to ban the former and circumscribe the latter.

3

The Airport Problem

A locational service conveys something from one geo-
graphical location to another. Examples are the transport
of persons or goods by air, land or water; posts and telecommunications; TV and radio; and the supply of water,
gas and electricity. . . . From the standpoint of public policy, their primary characteristic is a tendency to natural
monopoly. Provision of locational services usually requires
specialised routes (roads, rails, cables, pipes, satellites. . .)
and/or specialised apparatus for transmitting and receiving
(telephone exchanges, railway stations, airports, ports and
harbours. . .).

There might in principle be an approximation of perfect competition between *users* of these facilities—for
example, between the owners of taxi cabs, ships, or aircraft.
Typically, however, somewhere in the complex of factors
required for the provision of such services, there is a large
lump which cannot even in principle be reduced to perfect
competition.

There is a variety of regulatory responses to this problem. Public ownership probably is the most common.
Roads, ports and harbours, and airports, for example, are
very often owned and operated by one or another level of
government. The services themselves are frequently supplied by governments or their agencies (PTTs, electricity and
gas supply, rail and air transport), or are directly regulated
by them. (Hindley 1989, 223)

Airports illustrate the general phenomenon noted in the quotation above. They are, at best, imperfectly competitive, even in

large cities (for example, London or New York) with several
nearby airports.[6]

How best to deal with that situation is not of direct concern in the context of liberalization of international air transport.
Two possible responses, however—regulation and government
ownership—both raise problems for liberalization.

Slots

The basic issue can be formulated in terms of "slots." A slot gives a
carrier access to gates and runways at a particular airport at a particular time. To offer a schedule on a route, a carrier needs a slot at
the departure airport, and then, at an appropriate later time, at the
airport of destination. Some airports have unused runway space
and passenger and/or cargo handling facilities available at all or
most times. Others do not, including many of those important in
international air transport. When more slots are demanded than an
airport can supply, those available must be allocated among carriers
in some way, and some will be denied slots.

From an economic standpoint, the virtue of liberalization is
that it allows the most efficient providers of a service to expand
their market share. The liberalization of international air transport
therefore requires slots to be allocated in such a way that foreign
carriers who offer a more attractive service than domestic carriers
can obtain the slots they need to expand their market share.

Efficiency and Fairness. Two considerations are especially important in slot allocation. Economic efficiency is one. Efficiency
requires slots to be allocated among carriers in such a way that
they serve those passengers or shippers of freight who value them
most highly. It also calls for slots to be created until the marginal
social cost of a slot at a particular location equals its marginal social
benefit.

Fairness is also a central issue, especially in the context of
international economic affairs, where governments are open to
accusations of favoring their conationals. Fairness requires slots

to be allocated among carriers of different nationalities in a way that is neutral with respect to nationality, and that is seen to be neutral. No agreement to liberalize air transport between countries A and B could long survive a belief on the part of A carriers or the government of A that slots at airports in B were being improperly withheld from A carriers and given to B carriers. Slots are essential to doing business, so a denial of slots to A carriers hands business opportunities to B carriers at the expense of A carriers.

Old-style bilaterals—and also some open-skies bilaterals—allocate a specific number of slots to foreign carriers. That resolves at least some issues that open the way to accusations of unfairness. It is, however, a flawed solution. In effect, it creates submarkets—one for A slots and one for B slots—that are isolated from one another. Hence, an A slot at a particular airport at a particular time may have a different value than a B slot at the same airport and the same time—a prima facie indication of economic inefficiency.

Slots and Liberalization. More important in the present context, however, international agreements that allocate a particular number of slots to foreign airlines subvert the economic point of liberalization, which requires that efficient foreign carriers (and, of course, efficient domestic carriers) be able to expand the services they offer. From this point of view, an unbiased *process* of allocation is better than a fixed number of slots.

There are a number of such processes. In the United States, slots have sometimes been allocated through lotteries (known in the industry as slotteries). A fair lottery is certainly unbiased, but it allocates slots to carriers who are lucky, not to ones who are efficient. Of course, if slots once won can be resold, they may end up in the hands of the most efficient carriers. But in that case, there is a question as to why they were allocated by lottery in the first place. In these circumstances, a lottery seems merely to be a means of creating windfall gains for lucky carriers.

Economists asked to find an unbiased selection process, therefore, are unlikely to favor lotteries. They are more likely to advocate an open auction, with no favors given to any bidder.

Profit-Maximizing Airports? Behind that thought, however—at least in the minds of economists who know little about aviation—often lurks the idea of privately owned, profit-maximizing airports. The implicit model is one in which airports are operated for profit, and slots are inputs in the strategy of the private owners of an airport to maximize their profits. The management of the airport decides whether to sell slots outright or to rent them. If they are rented, the airport decides on the length of the lease. Airports might combine sales or leases of slots with other charges, such as a fee for landing (but the higher the landing fees, the lower the price of a slot). An airport might decide to charge only landing fees.

An immediate problem with this model, though, is that it fails to describe the ownership of airports accurately. Airports are sometimes privately owned, but are more usually owned and operated by one or another level of government, or by quasi-governmental bodies, which may have different objectives than maximizing profit.

Actual Slot Allocation. In reality, slot allocation is typically very different from that suggested by the airport-industry model. In the United States and the EU, for example, a large element of administrative discretion enters into the allocation of new slots. Many slots are de facto owned by existing airlines through historic use (they are, in the terminology, "grandfathered"), though this is subject to rules on use ("use it or lose it"). And slots can be bought and sold, though sometimes only by circuitous means. Slot allocation, in short, is neither fish nor fowl—neither a purely market matter nor a purely administrative matter.

A report by Kevin Done in the *Financial Times* conveys some of the flavor of slot arrangements at London's Heathrow Airport:

> British Airways' slot exchange deal with SN Brussels Airlines sheds a rare shaft of light into the opaque world of the grey market in take-off and landing slots at London's Heathrow airport.

Heathrow is the world's busiest international airport, and there are virtually no free take-off and landing slots available during most operating hours.

There is no open trading of slots, and prime slots only change hands through the so-called grey market, in which slots ostensibly are "exchanged." Prime slots are swapped for unattractive slots at commercially uninteresting times of day in return for a (normally undisclosed) payment.

Working out the going rate for a slot is a black art, but one leading airline executive said a peak hour pair of slots with a morning arrival before 9am could be worth up to $6m for some carriers, if they provided slots in both summer and winter schedules.

"Early morning arrival slots for flights from the U.S. or the Far East are like gold dust," he said.

Take-off and landing slots are mysterious assets. It is not clear who owns them. They do not turn up as assets valued in any company's balance sheet. Airports could be said to create them, airlines use them and give them value, and governments appear to regard them as some sort of "public good."

Under European regulations airlines have grand-father rights to use their slots. Under the so-called "use them or lose them" rule, they can hold on to them in perpetuity, as long as they use them for 80 per cent of a given season.

Trading in slots is carried on in a grey market because the 1993 European regulation was ambiguously drafted. It has been under almost permanent review ever since. The regulation does not allow the outright transfer of slots from one airline to another except through a partial or complete take-over of the company. The regulation does allow airlines to "exchange" slots, however.

In the case of the BA/SN Brussels deal, it is understood that BA first applied for and was granted some "worthless" unused slots at around 2300. It then "exchanged" these slots for the Belgian carrier's highly prized prime time slots, while an unspecified amount of money changed hands together with a commercial alliance agreement to sweeten the deal. SN Brussels can then cancel the "worthless" slots and they return to the pool.

> Other deals can be even more complicated. In theory, slots cannot be swapped between airports. But in a deal with Balkan Bulgarian Airlines earlier this year, BA effectively obtained Balkan's slots at Heathrow while Balkan received some slots from BA at Gatwick. In practice the airlines agreed two discrete deals with separate "exchanges" at each airport. (Done 2002)

In the United States, the buying and selling of slots has been legal since 1983, but the exact status of what is bought and sold is still unclear. Federal Aviation Authority (FAA) regulations treat a slot as a privilege, not a right. U.S. legislation appears to treat slots uniformly as an operating privilege granted by the FAA.

There is an obvious tension between the right of a carrier to buy and sell slots and the apparent right of the FAA to withdraw the use of the slot from a carrier. Lawyers discuss whether U.S. law (in particular, that deriving from the Fifth Amendment to the Constitution, which forbids the government to take property from citizens without proper compensation) would allow carriers to claim compensation successfully, were the FAA to withdraw slots from them. So far, this discussion lacks decisive cases or conclusions.

The European Commission has recently been trying to tidy up the ambiguous EU regulations referred to in the quotation above. It is reported that the Commission was on the point of authorizing open buying and selling of slots, but in the end bowed to existing interests. Instead of a market in slots, the Commission adopted a regulation that tightens the use-it-or-lose-it rules and requires incumbents to give up slots to new entrants.

Implications for Liberalization. The ambiguous legal nature of slots and the possibility of administrative intervention in their allocation create major difficulties for the liberalization of air transport. Genuine liberalization is blocked if successful carriers, foreign or domestic, cannot expand their operations. Genuine liberalization, that is to say, requires some means by which successful carriers can obtain more slots.

In principle, that could be done by official action. Official action, though, risks tension. Foreign carriers are likely to maintain—and sometimes rightly so—that domestic authorities unduly favor domestic airlines. Official power over slot allocation is therefore likely to make liberalization a more difficult exercise than it needs to be. In the light of that fact, it is worth returning to the airport industry model.

The Airport Industry Model Again

Private ownership of airports—or government ownership that tries to mimic the way private owners would behave—faces a number of problems. These now require more detailed discussion. It is necessary to make a judgment as to whether international aviation can be released from the problems posed by government control of airports.

Competition. As already noted, airports are imperfectly competitive. There is at least one solution to this problem, however, and it is relatively simple: regulate the airport industry.

In principle, airport regulators have straightforward rules open to them. First, an airport should be allowed to charge any price (landing fees and/or slot rental) at a particular time as long as its facilities continue to be fully used at that price and time. If it has spare capacity, the airport should not be allowed to charge a price higher than the marginal cost of using airport facilities. This rule, of course, is likely to mean different prices at different times of the day. Second, if new capacity can be created at a social cost that is less than the price carriers are prepared to pay for it, it should be created.

Much discussion of airport pricing centers on the question of who should receive the scarcity rents commanded by the airport. If airports sell slots, they receive the scarcity rents. If carriers are given slots without being required to pay, they receive them. The profits of airports and airlines evidently will not be the same in these two situations. Passengers, however, will be in essentially the same position whether carriers or airports obtain the rents.

The price of slots or airport services is not the only competition issue raised by the imperfectly competitive situation of airports. Domination of an airport by a single carrier, and the need to ensure that potential new entrants can acquire the slots they need to become actual entrants, are also issues. Various rules are suggested to deal with such problems: that a carrier can have no more than X percent of the slots at an airport, for example; or that Y percent of the slots at an airport should be auctioned each year.

This is not the place to discuss such issues, save to comment that seen from the perspective of the liberalization of international air transport, the problems require solutions that do not favor domestic carriers against foreign carriers. That such a requirement will impede the implementation of solutions seems unlikely. Indeed, that a satisfactory solution will call for discrimination against foreign carriers seems very unlikely.

Environment. Airports raise environmental issues, especially concerning noise. People living in the vicinity of an airport often demand restrictions on the number of landings and takeoffs, or bans on flight arrivals or departures at particular times—between the hours of 11 p.m. and 6 a.m., for example. The question of how to cope with aircraft noise is complicated, but it does not bear directly on the issues discussed here since, to a first approximation, foreign-owned and domestically owned aircraft are likely to create much the same noise. Policies to deal with noise, moreover, are unlikely to conflict with the rules above.

The existence of the environmental problem does say that the relevant cost of expanding airport capacity should be marginal *social* cost. Alternatively stated, it says that the costs of expanding airport facilities should include costs imposed upon persons who live or work in the vicinity of the airport.

Conclusions

Ownership and control of airports is a central issue in the liberalization of international civil aviation. Liberalization of the latter almost certainly cannot proceed without reform of the former.

Reform is not straightforward from a political point of view. In particular, incumbent carriers are likely to oppose it. When they have obtained the use of a slot without payment, they will not want to pay. When they have paid for the use of a slot, they will not want, as they might say, to pay twice. Nevertheless, it does not make much sense to talk about liberalization of international air transport without acknowledging the need to cut the Gordian knot of airport ownership and control.

4

The GATS and International Air Transport

Governments have very different attitudes toward the liberalization of international air transport. At one extreme are those that recognize the merits of liberalization and are willing to think seriously about it, though not necessarily to commit to it. At the other are those whose carriers could not survive increased competition, and who oppose liberalization unless it permits them to protect those carriers.

To satisfy both groups will be difficult. Some combination of safeguards and/or authorization of state aid may satisfy governments who want to protect their carriers. Others, however, might question the value of an agreement burdened with escape clauses and loopholes.

It may be easier to arrive at an agreement among the subset of WTO members who are interested in liberalization, leaving protectionist states with a largely undisturbed status quo. The much-discussed TCAA is one version of such a scheme. Typically, the TCAA is discussed as an option outside the WTO. A TCAA, however, is compatible with an application of the GATS to air transport. The point is discussed later in this chapter.

But while a global agreement might be difficult to reach, the idea is too attractive to abandon without exploration. Unless unanticipated changes in views occur, however, a global agreement will have to accommodate both protectionist and more liberal states. Application of the GATS to air transport services does not require, and is unlikely to be accompanied by, a universal renunciation of aviation protection.

This chapter, therefore, takes account of both positions. It discusses issues bearing on liberalization, but it also sets out means of protection. Membership in the GATS would permit governments to protect domestic carriers from foreign competition by means not currently used.

Structure of the GATS and Most-Favored-Nation Treatment

The GATS is not the strong agreement sought by supporters of the Uruguay Round negotiations on trade in services. Some central aspects of the institutions of the air transport industry and of national policies toward it—in particular the bilateral system—may conflict with the GATS. Others—in particular, those that discriminate between domestic and foreign carriers—are compatible with it.

Members of the WTO, all of whom accept the GATS, make two types of GATS commitments. The first is to adopt policies that conform to the general principles of the GATS framework and its annexes, such as most-favored-nation (MFN) treatment and national treatment. (The second is to make specific commitments with respect to particular sectors. The government of country A, for example, might commit itself to allow six foreign banks to enter the domestic market of country A in the next five years.)

Article II(1) of the GATS requires signatories to provide MFN treatment to other signatories, in words that stand as a definition:

> With respect to any measure covered by this Agreement, each Member shall accord immediately and unconditionally to services and service suppliers of any other Member treatment no less favourable than it accords to like services and service suppliers of any other country. (WTO 1995, 286)

The Bilateral System and MFN Status. The application to aviation of an unconditional MFN clause would almost certainly require an end of the bilateral system as currently practiced. The bilateral system is based on country A giving to country B concessions equivalent to those that B has given to A (in the view of A and B). The government of country A may or may not treat other countries similarly to B; the bilateral system does not require equal treatment of aviation partners.

MFN, however, does require equal treatment. Thus, what country A gives to country B under the A-B air service agreement, it must also give to countries C, D, and E. Under strict MFN and the GATS, moreover, the governments of countries C, D, and E could take legal action against country A in the WTO if A's treatment of B carriers was better than A's treatment of their carriers.

MFN Exemptions under the GATS. The GATS, however, does create an exception to strict MFN treatment. Article II(2) allows a member to "maintain a measure inconsistent with [MFN treatment] provided that such a measure is listed in, and meets the conditions of, the *Annex on Article II Exemptions*" (WTO 1995, 286).

The principal condition of an exemption is that the Council for Trade in Services (CTS) reviews all exemptions granted for more than five years. According to paragraph 4(a) of the *Annex*, the review will examine "whether the conditions which created the need for the exemption still prevail" (WTO 1995, 305). Neither the *Annex* nor the GATS itself, however, says how the CTS will arrive at its decisions, nor does either indicate what will happen if the CTS decides that the "conditions which created the need for the exemption" no longer prevail.

Paragraph 6 of the *Annex*, moreover, says that, "*In principle*, such exemptions shall not exceed the period of 10 years. *In any event*, they shall be subject to negotiation in subsequent trade liberalising rounds" (emphasis added) (WTO 1995, 305). The emphasized words seem to suggest that in practice, exemptions will extend beyond ten years.

For most sectors, this route to exemption from MFN treatment closed at the end of the Uruguay Round. Aviation, however, or at least the central issue of traffic rights—the conditions under which aircraft from a country can use aviation facilities in other countries—is in a singular position in this regard.[7]

Unique Position of Aviation

An *Annex to the GATS on Air Transport Services* removes air traffic rights from the GATS (WTO 1995, 307). Paragraph 2 of that *Annex* states:

> The Agreement, including its dispute settlement procedures, shall not apply to measures affecting:
> (a) traffic rights, however granted; or
> (b) services directly related to the exercise of traffic rights, except as provided in paragraph 3 of this Annex. (WTO 1995, 307)

Paragraph 3 of the *Annex on Air Transport Services* says that the GATS will apply to three ancillary areas: aircraft repair and maintenance, the selling and marketing of air transport services, and computer reservation systems (WTO 1995, 307). GATS disciplines apply to these services, therefore, and to any other ancillary service that is deemed not to be directly related to the exercise of traffic rights.[8] As far as traffic rights themselves are concerned, however, there is no ambiguity: no provision of the GATS applies to them.

This exemption has extensive implications. The United States and the EU (or, rather, its member states) are members of the WTO, and are therefore normally subject to MFN rules: if they extend trade concessions to one another, they are obliged to extend them to other WTO members as well. The exemption of aviation from the GATS, however, means that the United States and the EU could, if they wished, enter a TCAA-type agreement between themselves, wholly outside the GATS, without any obligation to provide similar freedoms to the carriers of other WTO members.

The exemption of air transport from the GATS, however, opens possibilities within the GATS. Though the route offered by the *Annex on Article II Exemptions* is closed to most other industries, for example, it is open to GATS members to apply the terms of that annex to new negotiations on air transport services.

Agreement on that issue would not necessarily be difficult to achieve. If exemptions from MFN treatment meant giving up rights to share the favorable treatment that the EU and United States gave to one another, other GATS members might be reluctant to allow them. In that circumstance, other members would give up a possible free ride by allowing exemptions. But the actual situation is that arrangements that the EU and the United States make between themselves with respect to aviation services create no valid claim of other GATS members to similar treatment. Hence, the possibility of free rides is limited or nonexistent, and there is little incentive to oppose application of the *Annex on Article II Exemptions* to new negotiations on air transport services within the GATS.

GATS-Compatible TCAA-Type Arrangements

The possibility of MFN exemptions opens the route to TCAA-type arrangements within the GATS. Members of the TCAA could simply use the exemption to avoid passing on to other GATS members concessions made to one another.

The *Annex on Article II Exemptions* might not be the best foundation for action, though. The words of the GATS bear repeating: "*In principle*, such exemptions shall not exceed the period of 10 years. *In any event*, they shall be subject to negotiation in subsequent trade liberalising rounds" (WTO 1995, 305). These words are so ambivalent as to raise the question of whether they have meaning. Can it safely be assumed, however, that they will *never* bite?

A plurilateral agreement—one that applies to the subset of WTO members that accept it—offers an alternative GATS-compatible route to an agreement that avoids the need to offer concessions to all members. Article II(3) of the *Agreement Establishing the WTO* (WTO 1995, 9–19) says that

> The agreements and associated legal instruments included in Annex 4 (hereinafter referred to as "Plurilateral Trade Agreements") are also part of this agreement for those Members that have accepted them, and are binding on

those Members. *The Plurilateral Trade Agreements do not create either obligations or rights for those Members that have not accepted them* [emphasis added]. (WTO 1995, 9–10)

It seems, therefore, that the United States and the EU could create within the GATS a plurilateral agreement on air transport services that would "not create either obligations or rights" for other WTO members. Thus, a TCAA could be constructed in the WTO without incurring MFN obligations to generalize the concessions entailed to other WTO members.

This route, however, has two drawbacks of its own. First, it would require the approval of other members of the WTO. Article X(9) of the *Agreement Establishing the WTO* says, "The Ministerial Conference, upon the request of the Members parties to a trade agreement, may decide *exclusively by consensus* to add that agreement to Annex 4 [that is, the *Annex for Plurilateral Trade Agreements*]" (emphasis added) (WTO 1995, 15).

Consensus on a plurilateral aviation agreement, however, might be relatively easy to achieve. The EU and the United States are in a legal position to make their arrangements outside of the WTO, without the approval of WTO members. They therefore have substantial bargaining strength on the issue within the WTO.

A second possible problem is that members of a plurilateral agreement cannot control its membership. They must accept as a member any WTO member that is willing and able to meet the conditions of entry. It is difficult to see, however, how the entry into the agreement of a WTO member that meets the conditions of entry could create a major problem.

What of countries outside the agreement, though? How would they relate to one another and to the members of the agreement, whether in the GATS or out of it?

If the TCAA were outside of the GATS, countries not belonging to the TCAA could negotiate bilaterals with other countries, as before. There is a question as to whether members of the TCAA would negotiate as individual countries or as a group, but that does not affect the general proposition.

If the GATS applies to air transport, the MFN rule makes the situation more difficult, in that it is harder to maintain the bilateral system. Perhaps it could be done by nonmembers of the TCAA taking extensive MFN exemptions, but the point of applying the GATS is unclear if it can be done only by giving so many exemptions that the GATS is emptied of content. An alternative, discussed below, is to shift to GATS-compatible modes of protection.

National Treatment

National treatment is often cited as the second cornerstone of the WTO (MFN treatment being the first). Article XVII of the GATS requires that

> In the sectors inscribed in its schedule, and subject to any conditions and qualifications set out therein, each Member shall accord to services and service suppliers of any other Member, in respect of all measures affecting the supply of services, treatment no less favourable than that it accords to its own like services and service suppliers. (WTO 1995, 298)

National treatment is defined by the words, "treatment no less favourable than that it accords to its own like services and service suppliers."

Article XVII, however, says that national treatment applies only to services in which a member has made a specific commitment. Even when such a commitment has been made, moreover, the member can avoid aspects of national treatment that it dislikes by appropriately inscribing conditions in its schedule (though these are then subject to negotiation). The national treatment provisions of the GATS are not strong.

So many current practices in national aviation policies violate national treatment that it might seem, at first blush, that national treatment would require as large an overhaul of industry practices as MFN treatment. But that is not so.

Examples of current practices and policies in national regulation of air transport services that are inconsistent with national treatment are:

- restrictions on foreign ownership of domestically based carriers;
- restrictions on access of foreign carriers to internal routes (cabotage);
- restrictions on the nationality of crew members on internal routes;
- requirements that government travelers use domestic carriers;
- prohibitions on wet leasing (that is, the renting of aircraft and crews) from foreigners; and
- methods of allocating takeoff and landing slots at airports.

The GATS does not prohibit any of these practices, however, nor any other instance of nonnational treatment. To maintain them, all that is required, even if specific commitments with respect to air transport services are undertaken, is to list them in the relevant schedule.

State Aid

A frequent argument for the bilateral system is that it is an effective means of dealing with competition from state-owned and state-subsidized airlines. The argument has resonance, especially in the United States. Privately owned U.S. airlines have historically had to compete with state-owned airlines elsewhere, at least some of which were subsidized by governments.

The problem cannot be denied. The difficulties in coping with state aid of the EU, even within its relatively homogenous jurisdiction and relatively strong legal structure, are a pertinent illustration.

Nor can it be denied that the bilateral system can eliminate or alleviate the effects of subsidies to publicly owned airlines on their competitors. What might be doubted is that the bilateral remedy is proportional to the problem. Does it make sense to deal with distortions of competition by eliminating competition?

The GATS as presently structured, however, does not offer a plausible alternative. Article XV of the GATS deals with subsidies, but the disciplines it prescribes cannot be described as harsh. It says that "members recognize that under certain circumstances, subsidies may have distortive effects on trade in services," and it calls upon members to "enter into negotiations with a view to developing the necessary multilateral disciplines to avoid such distortive effects" (WTO 1995, 296). So far, however, no such disciplines have appeared.

Article XV also says that "any Member which considers that it is adversely affected by a subsidy of another Member may request consultations with that Member on such matters. Such requests shall be accorded sympathetic consideration" (WTO 1995, 296).

These provisions are unlikely to allay the concerns of privately owned carriers asked to enter the GATS—that is, to enter an environment in which the effects of subsidies on competition may be considerably larger than they are in the present structure of the industry. It follows that one factor determining the enthusiasm with which such carriers regard the GATS will be the nature of the "necessary multilateral disciplines" that emerge from the negotiations on the subject promised by Article XV.

Dispute Settlement

Dispute settlement in the WTO provides a major focus for opposition to the idea of bringing aviation services into the GATS, especially in the United States. Members of the industry believe that existing dispute-settlement procedures in the industry are superior to those of the GATS, especially in terms of the time taken to resolve disputes. The subject is therefore worth extended discussion.

Dispute Settlement under the GATS. Article XXIII of the GATS allows a member to invoke WTO dispute-settlement procedures. These apply if the member

> should consider that any other Member fails to carry out its obligations or specific commitments under this Agreement . . . [or if] any benefit that it could reasonably have expected to accrue under a specific commitment of another Member is being nullified and impaired or . . . the attainment of any objective of the Agreement is being impeded as a result of the application of any measure which does not conflict with the provisions of this agreement. (WTO 1995, 301)

These grounds are very broad. In addition to violation of obligations or specific commitments, nullification and impairment that are a consequence of actions not in violation of the GATS may become the subject of dispute settlement. The penalties attached to nonviolation complaints, however, are weaker than for violations.

The report of the panel dealing with a complaint is accepted unless it is rejected by consensus. A party to a dispute can appeal against the finding of a panel, but the findings of the appellate body are also accepted unless rejected by consensus. A national government found to have nullified or impaired benefits due to another WTO member has essentially no chance of avoiding acceptance by the General Council of a finding to that effect.

A government found in violation of a WTO undertaking must either bring its policy or actions into conformity with WTO rules or face withdrawal by the injured member or members of concessions or other obligations that are equivalent to the nullification and impairment caused by the violation. Withdrawal of concessions need not occur in the sector in which the violation has occurred. A violation of an undertaking in services, for example, can be met with a penalty in the form of increased tariffs on goods exported from the transgressor. Article 22.3 of the *Understanding on Rules and Procedures Governing the Settlement of Disputes* (WTO 1995, 353–78) makes clear, however, that concessions should be withdrawn in the sector in which the violation occurred when that is feasible.

When nullification and impairment occur without violation of a WTO rule, members have the alternative of maintaining the measure but paying compensation for costs inflicted on trading partners. A government cannot be expected to commit itself to withdraw a measure that does not itself violate any WTO agreement.[9]

Timetable for WTO Disputes. All steps in the dispute-settlement procedure are subject to a strict timetable. Nevertheless, the total time taken in reaching a final decision in the WTO dispute is central to the hesitations of carriers in submitting themselves to it.

Article 20.1 of the *Understanding* says that:

> Unless otherwise agreed to by the parties to the dispute, the period from the establishment of the Panel by the DSB [Dispute Settlement Body] until the DSB considers the panel or appellate report for adoption shall not as a general rule exceed nine months where the report is not appealed or twelve months where the report is appealed. (WTO 1995, 366)

However, consultations are required before a panel is requested. This can take up to sixty days. Moreover, delays in implementing recommendations can be substantial. Hence, the period between initiation of a dispute and the implementation of remedies can exceed a year, and may sometimes take much more.

Aviation Procedures. Most problems under air service bilaterals are resolved directly between the airline and the foreign government or informally between governments. If such means fail, the dispute-settlement procedures in U.S. bilaterals, for example, typically permit an aggrieved party to invoke expedited consultations (within thirty to sixty days). If the issue is still unresolved after consultations, the aggrieved party is free to submit the dispute to arbitration.

A number of nations, including the United States, take the position that under such circumstances, a nation may take steps to protect its position and preserve the relative benefits from its agreement until the dispute is resolved. These measures could include the withdrawal of route rights or lesser restrictions on carriers designated by the other party to the dispute.

As a practical matter, the bilateral aviation dispute-resolution system has led to few arbitration proceedings. The process has encouraged the resolution of disputes without the need to resort to the formal dispute-resolution process. The ability of aviation authorities to impose restrictions has apparently been tempered by the bureaucratic cost of doing so. Similarly, inconvenience to travelers (and hence voters), the mutual vulnerability of airline operations to government sanctions, and the high level of political visibility inherent in retaliatory exchanges appear to have raised the cost of such fighting high enough to encourage airlines and governments to resolve air-service disputes by less confrontational means.

Compatibility of Dispute-Settlement Systems. The compatibility of these two procedures may not be germane to any real world issue. The aviation dispute-settlement procedure is designed to adjudicate differences over the interpretation of bilateral agreements. If air transport services entered the GATS, it is probable that the bilateral system would be abandoned.

It is worth noting, though, that the two procedures are not as dissimilar as they might at first sight appear. For example, both require a consultation period of approximately the same length. And there is no obvious reason why the arbitration procedure of the aviation model should not be assimilated to the panel procedure of the Dispute Settlement Understanding (DSU).[10]

Were air transport services to enter the GATS, however, the Appellate Body of the WTO would be the final authority. The aviation industry, especially in the United States, might find that difficult to accept, and it would almost certainly be a sticking point for WTO members.

GATS-Compatible Protection

Much discussion of liberalizing the provision of aviation services, especially among members of domestic industries, focuses on the withdrawal of policies that protect those industries. It is therefore pertinent to note that the GATS offers two protective instruments not currently deployed in aviation that are compatible with its national treatment and MFN provisions. One of these is the application of overall quotas to air traffic; the other is a tariff.

Overall Quotas. Under the GATS, a country can impose an overall numerical restriction on international flights if MFN is applied to the allocation of shares of that quota. Article XVI of the GATS ("market access") provides a list of restrictions "which a member shall not maintain or adopt . . . unless otherwise specified in its schedule." The list includes "limitations on the number of service providers . . . in the form of numerical quotas"; "limitations on the total value of service transactions . . . in the form of numerical quotas"; and "limitations on the total number of service operations . . . in the form of quotas" (WTO 1995, 297). These may or may not preclude an overall quantitative limit on flights into or out of a country. The issue, though, bears only upon the question of whether the quota must be specified in a country's schedule. That an overall quota can legally be imposed is quite clear.

A country can therefore retain numerical controls on incoming flights by establishing a global quota on the number of flights permitted. Moreover, so long as shares of that quota are allocated to other countries in some manner deemed to be nondiscriminatory (an issue, of course, inevitably open to dispute), the control is compatible with MFN treatment.

Such a system might seem similar to the traditional bilateral system, at least insofar as the flights permitted under a country's bilateral deals can be added up to arrive at an aggregate number of permitted flights. Under the traditional bilateral system, however, the aggregate total of flights is built up from components designed to produce equality between what is given and received by partners within each pair of countries. A global quota would be allocated on the basis of one partner receiving the same treatment as another. The two systems would be equivalent only in exceptional circumstances.

A system based on global quotas, moreover, may produce perverse outcomes. Country C might try to liberalize, for example, and expand its global quota. But if country D simultaneously reduces its global quota, the net effect may be that C's more generous quota fails to expand the total number of flights on C-D routes, while merely increasing the share of them going to the airline of protectionist state D or to some third state. Trying to combine MFN treatment with a quota system does not yield clear and obvious advantages over the bilateral system as it currently exists, either from the standpoint of supporters of the bilateral system or the GATS.

Tariffs. Air transport, though, has a feature that is unusual in service industries: the visibility of the service as it is delivered. Many services are "invisible"—customs officials cannot easily detect them as they cross the border (for example, an appendicitis operation or a financial transaction). When a service transaction is invisible, border measures are not an effective means of protecting local providers of the service. A Boeing 747, though, is highly visible. It is therefore technically feasible to employ border measures with respect to imports of air transport services. Taxes on arrivals of foreign aircraft would be directly equivalent to tariffs on imports.

Such "tariffs" would probably improve upon the bilateral system. In trade in goods it is normally possible to devise a set of tariffs and subsidies that improves upon a quota regime; that is, that makes it possible for all affected parties to be better off. A similar result is likely to apply to aviation services.

Conclusion on Aviation Services and the GATS

There are scant grounds for optimism about bringing the central issue of air traffic rights into the GATS in the near future.

There is, on the other hand, considerable scope for identifying those services that are not "directly related to the exercise of air traffic rights," to which the GATS already applies, in principle. That would be valuable not only in itself, but also in providing the aviation community with reasons for a closer acquaintance with the GATS.

The difficulty in bringing air traffic rights into the GATS is not primarily due to the difficulties of fitting into the GATS aviation policies that violate national treatment. Such policies present no problem at all, at least insofar as the GATS as an institution is concerned. (They may, of course, create difficulties with partners in an actual negotiation.)

The real difficulties are likely to lie elsewhere. They are the issues of slot allocation and airports, subsidies, and, probably most important, the likely difficulties of persuading U.S. carriers, in particular, to accept the supremacy of the WTO dispute-settlement system.

Leaving aside dispute settlement, these problems are not, in principle, insuperable. It is easy to think of a new agreement on aviation services that would set out rules for dealing with them. The problem lies in the substance. There is little sign of agreement among the major aviation powers on how the issues should be dealt with. Thus, there is a major problem quite apart from the complication created by the fact that some WTO members regard protection of the domestic flag carrier as the primary objective of their aviation policy.

Dispute settlement, on the other hand, raises difficulties that may prove to be insuperable. On the one hand, there is no possibility of air transport services entering the GATS without becoming subject to WTO dispute-settlement procedures, even if only in the final stages of a dispute. On the other hand, there is little prospect that the U.S. air transport industry will willingly accept the supremacy of the WTO in this regard. If the U.S. government allows the U.S. industry a de facto power of veto, therefore, a GATS agreement on aviation services is unlikely.

5

Cargo and Express Delivery

If bringing the whole air transport industry into the GATS is too difficult, would a viable alternative be for a part of it to enter, perhaps blazing a trail for the rest to follow in due course? Some possibilities along these lines are presented by cargo and express-delivery services.

All-Cargo Services

According to the WTO,

> It would seem that in general, the regime accorded to cargo flights, whether bilaterally or unilaterally, may be more liberal than that for passenger flights. States which did not have all-cargo carriers, but which did have traders needing air cargo services beyond what their national airline could provide through combination services were not reluctant to authorise all-cargo operations, which could often operate at off-peak times and at uncongested airports, thus minimising airport capacity problems. Thus, because many States saw no need to protect their national airlines from all-cargo competitors, and found some benefit in authorising such services, all-cargo services were rarely regulated as such. (WTO 1998, 34)

This de facto more liberal treatment of all-cargo services can, perhaps, be translated into a GATS agreement covering them. While such an agreement would still need to surmount the problems noted in the previous chapter, the process might be easier.

A negotiation on all-cargo flights, however, faces an additional problem. A great deal of cargo—60 percent of the total—is carried in the belly holds of passenger aircraft (WTO 1998, 34). Such combination carriers might see an agreement on all-cargo services as a threat. They might, for example, oppose a proposal to lift restrictions on all-cargo operations that did not extend to their own belly-cargo operations. Hostility from that substantial part of the air cargo industry would not bode well for an agreement on all-cargo services.

An attempt to create an agreement on all-cargo flights therefore faces a delicate problem of balance. If the agreement is to be worth doing, it must create advantages for all-cargo carriers. On the other hand, it must avoid creating disadvantages for combination carriers. To fulfill both conditions at the same time may not be possible, in which case an all-cargo agreement may be beyond the skills of negotiators.

Express-Delivery Services

One aviation-intensive sector, however, gives larger grounds for optimism. International express delivery is a dynamic sector.

> There are about 70 companies that operate pure cargo services, 50 of which operate internationally. This market is estimated to be worth U.S. $20 billion annually and could triple in size by 2015. . . . The sector is characterised by competition between traditional suppliers (forwarding agents and airline companies) and the express delivery companies, known as "integrators.". . . Traditional suppliers, though they still account for some 94 per cent of the market, are tending to lose ground to the express delivery companies, which operate much more quickly and are moving up from express mail and packages to heavier cargoes. Some forecasts suggest that the market share of the traditional suppliers could fall to 70 per cent or less by 2013. (The share of integrators in the U.S. market rose from 10 per cent in 1984 to 84 per cent today). The market is growing by seven to eight per cent a year. (WTO 1998, 34)

Jimmy Reyna, a well-known trade attorney, provides a comment on the scale of the U.S. express-delivery industry. He observes that in the United States,

> the sector employs more than 400,000 people and earns more than $45 billion in combined annual revenue. . . . [Express delivery companies] operate more than 1000 aircraft and 184,000 vehicles, and daily deliver more than 4.1 million packages by air to more than 211 countries. In addition, the sector contributes significantly to the economies of other countries—the two largest U.S. companies [in the sector] employ more than 50,000 people outside the United States. (Reyna 1998, 4)

Problem of Definition. A first problem, however, is definition. The idea that there should be negotiations on express-delivery services is based on the perception that governments may be prepared to offer concessions to providers of such services that they are not willing to offer to air freight in general. Probably that is true, as discussed below. But a proposal to negotiate about just one part of an industry presupposes that the part nominated for negotiation can be distinguished from the rest.

This is not mere linguistic pedantry. If the rest can easily acquire the features deemed to distinguish the part, then a negotiation that purports to be about that part is in fact about the whole industry. A negotiation about the treatment of aircraft that are painted blue is a negotiation about every aircraft whose owner will paint it blue, given sufficient inducement. That may be close to all aircraft—and a negotiation about the treatment of blue aircraft therefore cannot avoid the problems that would attend a negotiation about all aircraft.

A willingness to make concessions for express delivery will be difficult to translate into policy without making a distinction between air freight and express delivery that is legally viable. Without such a distinction, express delivery cannot be detached from air freight in general, and if the problems of negotiating about air freight prove insoluble, as they may, those problems will also block the separate-negotiation route to improving international treatment of express-delivery services.

Express-delivery operators have sought to distinguish their industry from air cargo in general, citing properties such as "time-definite"; "time-sensitive"; "just-in-time delivery"; "door-to-door"; and "integrated." At first sight, these characteristics do seem to distinguish express-delivery services from air freight in general. On closer inspection, the characteristics seem less decisive. It seems likely that any air freight carrier could acquire these characteristics, given sufficient inducement. Hence, a negotiation about a sector defined in these terms may have to confront the difficulties that would face a negotiation on air freight.[11]

Even a worst-case scenario along these lines, however, leaves intact many of the grounds for optimism about express delivery in the GATS. Too tight a focus on finding characteristics that distinguish express delivery from air freight in general misses a central point about express-delivery services in the GATS context: While express-delivery services are aviation intensive, the service of express delivery is an activity distinct from the provision of air transport services as such.

Perhaps air transport services or air freight services can be liberalized in the GATS. So much the better for them if so, and so much the better for express-delivery services. Even if they cannot, however, that is not the end of the GATS road for international express-delivery services.

Express Delivery and Telecoms. Express-delivery services share many of the characteristics of telecoms—the one being concerned with efficient and speedy transmission of voice and data, the other with rapid transmission of physical things. The factors that lay behind the success of the GATS telecoms negotiation[12]—notably the fact that many developing countries recognized that an efficient telecoms service sharply improved their prospects of attracting foreign investment—therefore hold the prospect of pushing negotiations on express-delivery services to a successful conclusion.

Many of the technical problems faced by express delivery and telecoms are similar also, and both privately owned telecoms providers and express delivery providers must operate in areas that are, or traditionally have been, dominated by state-owned monopolies. Indeed, they must often compete with the same state-owned monopolies, in the shape of postal, telegraph, and telephone organizations (PTTs).

This link between telecoms and express delivery may be valuable to express-delivery operators. One outcome of the GATS telecoms negotiation was a code on competition between, and regulation of, telecoms providers: the so-called *Reference Paper*, which is discussed below. It seems likely that some of the principles of the *Reference Paper* can also be applied to express-delivery services.

Before discussing that issue, however, the problems of competition in the postal sector call for exploration.

Facilitating Express Delivery

Providers of express-delivery services have a clear idea of what they would like a GATS negotiation to achieve in areas outside aviation. This has two principal components, both of which are readily justified in broader terms of social welfare. One is to put an end to inconsistent and arbitrary customs procedures. The second is to set the terms of competition between providers of express-delivery services and national post offices in ways that do not give too great an advantage to the latter.

These two broad components can be divided into more detailed targets, each of which, of course, reflects a current problem. The industry would like:

- removal of restrictions on the weight and value of express shipments;
- measures to avoid unnecessary delays from customs clearance procedures;
- removal of restrictions on cargo handling—in particular, regulations that force express carriers to use local handling companies' carriers rather than their own personnel to transport express shipments from baggage collection areas to customs clearance areas;

- disciplines on arbitrary revaluation of the declared value of shipments by customs; and
- regularization of charges and fees imposed on express shipments.

Customs Clearance Procedures. Customs clearance procedures are not, of course, a problem only for express delivery. Trade facilitation, much of which is concerned with custom clearance issues, was one of the so-called "Singapore issues," which were the proximate cause of the collapse of the Cancun meeting of the WTO. It is the least controversial of them, however, and will almost certainly appear on the agenda of a revived round. So far as this class of problem is concerned, therefore, express-delivery providers are likely to face an open door.

Competition with National Post Offices.
Nontariff barriers. Express-delivery operators complain that governments support their public postal operators (PPOs) by a variety of nontariff means, placing unreasonable conditions and restrictions on the activities of the express-delivery operators. A government might fix the terms on which foreign express-delivery providers may compete, for example; or it might impose taxes on providers of express-delivery services (sometimes using the proceeds to subsidize the PPOs).

The provisions of the GATS for MFN treatment and/or its national treatment provisions would address many problems in this class. Where this is true, the solution lies not in establishing new GATS disciplines or annexes, but rather in persuading offending governments to accept existing provisions of the GATS and to make specific commitments in relevant sectors.

Unfair competition: PPOs. Most governments give to their national PPOs a monopoly over delivery of certain types of letters and parcels. This gives rise to two potential problems. The first is that particular services may be designated as the exclusive domain of a PPO even though they could be better performed by a competitor. The second is that PPOs might use such de jure monopolies as a basis for the creation of de facto monopolies in other areas.

The problems that the operations of PPOs pose for express delivery are more difficult than those posed by customs clearance. In part, that is because public mail service raises matters of principle not presented by nontariff barriers and customs procedures (assuming, perhaps optimistically, that no one supports in principle customs procedures that are slow, arbitrary, and inefficient). But it is also true that cross-subsidization—the essential issue in the alleged extension of PPO monopolies—is more difficult to detect and prove than difficulties with customs clearance.

National postal monopolies. A PPO is typically required to maintain a universal service at a standard charge; that is, it is required to collect letters and packages from, or deliver them to, any address in its country, with no variation in price by origin or destination. (Prices may, of course, vary with weight and class of service.) The exclusive rights to provide particular services that are given to many PPOs derive from this requirement of universal service at a standard charge.

Some collections and deliveries cost more than others. Some are likely to cost less than the standard charge, while others cost more. When a PPO has a monopoly on collection and delivery, it can use the profits derived from packages and letters whose collection and delivery cost less than the standard charge to pay for its losses on those that cost more. The universal service obligation of the typical PPO is financed by cross-subsidization.

PPO monopoly is necessary to this result. Competition for collection and delivery, the argument goes, would result in competitors' skimming the cream out of this system. They would bid away from PPOs collections and deliveries whose cost was less than the standard charge, leaving the PPO with only high-cost-of-delivery items—and unable to cover the cost of its remaining operations.

This argument for granting a monopoly to PPOs is far from impregnable. In the first place, the idea of universal postal service at charges that do not vary by point of collection or delivery is open to challenge. The theory of universal postal service at a standard charge holds that persons who live in inaccessible places should pay the same for postal services as people who live in more accessible locations. Presumably that proposition is based upon the notion that such a policy helps to bind together the members of a nation. Whether or not uniform postal charges once had that effect, however, the idea may have a bizarre appearance to modern eyes. Certainly the idea is not applied to other services that might be expected to perform the same function. Governments—at least the governments of moderately large countries—do not usually insist on a standard telephone charge for calls within their countries, for example, nor that the transport of persons within the country should cost the same, regardless of the distance traveled.[13]

But even if it is accepted that the postal services of persons in less accessible places are to be subsidized, the traditional PPO solution still faces a major problem. The proposition that the subsidy is best financed by charges on other mail that are higher than the costs of collecting and delivering that other mail is difficult to defend. A tax on a single good—in this case, on mail whose cost of collection and delivery is relatively low—is an expensive way of raising revenue from a social standpoint. An alternative would be to allow competition for delivery and collection but to offer subsidies for delivery to and collection from inaccessible locations. Such subsidies could be financed from general tax revenue.

A PPO that is allowed to finance its universal service by cross-subsidization, moreover, both collects the "tax"—in the form of the higher-than-necessary charge on low-cost collection and delivery—and uses the revenue derived from it. That invites diversion of the revenue to other uses—for example, providing an easy life for PPO staff.[14]

Whatever the strength of its rationale, however, the existence of PPO monopolies in the delivery of certain classes of letters and packets raises two issues for public policy. They are:

- the proper extent of the legal monopoly given to PPOs; and
- the prevention of "monopoly creep"—the tendency of PPOs to extend their legal monopoly to services in which they have not been granted a monopoly (for example, by subsidizing express services from the profits of normal mail services).

Proper extent of PPO monopoly. The merits of the case for any PPO monopoly are open to doubt. It follows that nonarbitrary answers to the question of the proper extent of the monopoly will be difficult or impossible to find.

It is useful, however, to formulate the issue as an incremental problem. This entails posing the question: if the purpose of the PPO monopoly is X, can that justify its extension to activity Y? If the ultimate purpose of a universal postal service at prices undifferentiated by the regions of a country is to bind members of the nation together, for example, is it possible to question whether a PPO monopoly should extend to mail sent to and from foreign destinations?

In defense of a PPO monopoly in foreign mail collection and delivery, it might be argued that the ability to send mail to foreign countries at prices that do not vary by regions of the country of dispatch is just another aspect of binding the members of the nation. But whatever the plausibility of that proposition for internal mail, it is clearly less when applied to foreign mail; and since the proposition might be thought to have little plausibility for internal mail, it might be thought to have none at all for foreign mail. This is not to suggest that PPOs should not handle foreign mail—only that a case for a PPO to have *an exclusive right* to handle foreign mail, or any class of foreign mail, is weak.

An alternative defense of a PPO monopoly in the collection and delivery of foreign mail is that it is needed to finance domestic operations. In effect, that is to suggest that a PPO should be enabled to tax foreign mail in order to subsidize its domestic operations. Many persons, though, will regard letters between domestic residents and foreign residents as being as important as letters between domestic residents. The proposal that one should be taxed to subsidize the other is unlikely to win universal assent.

Costs and benefits form a second criterion when thinking in terms of increments in a PPO's exclusive rights. A PPO with exclusive rights to an activity may charge a price that is greatly in excess of cost or of the price at which others would be willing to provide the service. In that event, the question of whether the exclusive right provides benefits commensurate with its costs to users must arise.

That question is not an easy one to answer in these circumstances, in which the alleged benefit ("binding members of the nation together") comes close to mysticism and is difficult or impossible to quantify. Presumably, however, there is some level of charges to users that so far exceeds the costs or the prices at which others would undertake the activity that even the most fervent advocate of universal postal service would agree that the activity should be opened to competition.

Combating extensions of PPO monopolies. Combating extensions of PPO monopoly is not merely a problem for the GATS. In the first place, a number of private legal actions are going forward, involving the governments of the United States, Canada, and Germany (through the European Commission) as defendants. The complaint in all three cases is that these governments have subsidized their PPOs and/or allowed them to practice cross-subsidization. The plaintiff in all three cases is UPS (Brooks 2000).

The European Commission is at the forefront of efforts to deal with the problem by means of international organizations. As part of the process of creating a single market, the European Union has undertaken internal reform of its postal services. As in other cases of liberalization (trade in services, for example), the EU provides a laboratory for the rest of the world, highlighting, even in the relatively homogeneous setting of the EU, problems that are likely to attend broader-based efforts in the GATS.

The GATS as yet has no direct experience in dealing with postal and courier services. A number of precedents, though, might serve as platforms for an agreement on these services.

PPOs in the European Community. The current Community leg-islation on postal services is Directive 97/67/EU of December 15, 1997 (European Community 1998). Its key points anticipate those that might arise in a negotiation in the GATS.

Universal service. The universal service provisions of the directive specify what must be available to citizens, not what is reserved to PPOs. Article 3(3) lays down that the universal service shall include a minimum of one clearance and one delivery per day, for at least five days a week. As Article 3(4) requires,

> Each Member State shall adopt the measures necessary to ensure that the universal service includes the following minimum facilities:
> - the clearance, sorting, transport and distribution of postal items up to two kilograms,
> - the clearance, sorting, transport and distribution of postal packages up to ten kilograms,
> - services for registered items and insured items. (European Community 1998)

Reserved services. The areas in which services may be reserved are defined by Article 7(1) and 7(2):

> 1. To the extent necessary to ensure the maintenance of universal service, the services which may be reserved by each Member State for the universal service provider(s) shall be the clearance, sorting, transport and delivery of items of domestic correspondence, whether by accelerated delivery or not, the price of which is five times the public tariff for an item of correspondence in the first weight step of the fastest standard category where such category exists, pro-vided that they weigh less than 350 g[rams].
> 2. To the extent necessary to ensure the maintenance of universal service, cross-border mail and direct mail may continue to be reserved within the price and weight limits laid down in paragraph 1. (European Community 1998)

Article 7(3) foresaw that "the European Parliament and the Council [should] decide not later than 1 January 2000 . . . on the further gradual and controlled liberalisation of the postal market . . . as well as a further review of the price and weight limits, with effect from 1 January 2003" (European Community 1998).

This timetable was disrupted by the resignation of the Santer Commission in March 1999, and it is now widely assumed that the effective date of further reductions in price and weight limits will be 2005. The general thrust of the program, however, is to set limits on the reserved services and then to reduce the limits.

The 350-gram limit, however, would open up only 3 percent of the European letter market. The Commission was rumored to want to reduce the limit to fifty grams, which would open up 27 percent of the existing market. PPOs, however, are lobbying strongly for a new upper limit of 150 grams.

Cost accounting. An obvious problem in coming to grips with cross-subsidization is to demonstrate that it is actually in practice. One way of doing this is to insist upon the adoption by PPOs of more accurate and targeted accounting practices. Article 14(2) of the Directive provides for the establishment of cost accounting systems for post offices:

> The universal service providers shall keep separate accounts within their internal accounting systems at least for each of the services within the reserved sector on the one hand and for the non-reserved services on the other. The accounts for the non-reserved services should clearly distinguish between services which are part of the universal service and services which are not. Such internal accounting systems shall operate on the basis of consistently applied and objectively justifiable cost accounting principles. (European Community 1998)

Rules are set out for the assignment of common costs in Article 14(3) of the Directive. The Organisation for Economic Co-operation and Development (OECD), however, is skeptical of the value of these:

Many countries (following the EU postal directive) require accounting separation of the competitive and non-competitive activities of the incumbent's postal business as a mechanism for detecting cross-subsidisation. Often, this accounting separation relies on a form of "fully distributed cost" accounting (again, following the EU postal directive). The fully distributed cost approach does not yield economically meaningful results and will not yield a reliable price floor for detecting anti-competitive cross-subsidisation. In many cases the accounting and information gathering procedures of the public postal operators are not sufficiently rigorous. (OECD 1999, 7)

In formal terms, this must be correct. The EU, however, is at least trying to come to grips with the problems. Experience may well improve the manner in which it does so.

GATS Provisions and Precedents. A number of GATS articles or agreements are relevant to the problems posed by organizations such as PPOs. In particular, they deal with the possibility that these organizations might use profits from their legal monopolies to subsidize activities in which they have no exclusive rights. Mattoo (1997) gives a useful account of WTO disciplines in this area.

GATS Article VIII ("Monopolies and Exclusive Service Suppliers"). Article VIII of the GATS was introduced in chapter 3. Article VIII(1) requires members to "ensure that any monopoly supplier of a service in its territory does not . . . act in a manner inconsistent with the Member's obligations under Article II [that is, MFN] and specific commitments" (WTO 1995, 291); and Article VIII(2) calls on members to ensure that in the supply of services outside the scope of its monopoly rights, a "supplier does not abuse its monopoly position to act in its territory in a manner inconsistent with" the member's specific commitments (WTO 1995, 292). If a member believes that a monopoly supplier is behaving in a manner inconsistent with paragraph 1 or 2, "The Council for Trade in Services [CTS] may . . . request the Member establishing, maintaining or authorising such supplier to provide specific information concerning the relevant operations" (WTO 1995, 292).

As noted in chapter 3, these disciplines fall some way short of draconian. In the first place, Article VIII only applies where specific commitments have been made—it can be avoided entirely simply by the government's failing to make specific commitments in the relevant sector. In the second place, it is not clear what process follows a request by the CTS for "specific information concerning the relevant operations." Presumably, the government of a monopoly supplier that is in breach of obligations undertaken by the government can be taken to dispute settlement if it fails to rectify the situation; but, also presumably, this process cannot start until the CTS has played its role—whatever that is.

Telecoms Reference Paper. The WTO Telecommunications Accord produced an agreement that may be more pertinent than Article VIII. It is contained in the *Reference Paper*, subtitled "Regulatory Principles Adopted under the WTO Telecommunications Accord" (APEC 1997).[15] The *Reference Paper* is, of course, specific to telecoms. The question here is whether it sets a precedent that could be applied to other service industries, and in particular to the provision of express-delivery services.

The *Reference Paper* defines a major supplier as:

> a supplier which has the ability to materially affect the terms of participation (having regard to price and supply) in the relevant market for basic telecommunication services as a result of:
> (a) control over essential facilities; or
> (b) use of its position in the market. (APEC 1997)

Paragraph 1 then continues:

> 1. *Competitive safeguards*
> 1.1 *Prevention of anti-competitive practices in telecommunications*
>   Appropriate measures shall be maintained for the purpose of preventing suppliers who, alone or together, are a major supplier from engaging in or continuing anti-competitive practices.

1.2 *Safeguards*
  (a) The anti-competitive practices referred to above shall include in particular
  (b) engaging in anti-competitive cross-subsidisation
  (c) using information obtained from competitors with anti-competitive results; and
  (d) not making available to other service suppliers on a timely basis technical information about essential facilities and commercially relevant information which are necessary for them to provide services. (APEC 1997)

Paragraph 2 of the *Reference Paper* deals with interconnection, a problem less relevant to express-delivery providers than to telecoms providers. Paragraph 3, however, is directly relevant to express delivery:

3. *Universal service*
  Any member has the right to define the kind of universal service obligation it wishes to maintain. Such obligations will not be regarded as anti-competitive *per se,* provided that they are administered in a transparent, non-discriminatory and competitively neutral manner and are not more burdensome than necessary for the kind of universal service defined by the Member. (APEC 1997)

Paragraph 4 ("Public availability of licensing criteria") requires that when licensing is necessary, there will be transparency in the granting of licenses. Moreover, it calls for the reasons for the denial of a license to be "made known to the applicant upon request." (APEC 1997)

Clearly, provisions of this type have potential relevance to express-delivery providers. Governments accepting the paper are required to maintain "appropriate measures" to prevent cross-subsidization. If cross-subsidization can be shown to occur, therefore, it follows that the government's measures are not appropriate, and it is vulnerable to a violation complaint in the DSB.

Members are able to define their own level of universal service. The requirement that related obligations are "administered in a transparent, non-discriminatory and competitively neutral manner," and especially that they "are not more burdensome than necessary for the kind of universal service defined by the Member" nevertheless provides words and obligations that appear strong enough to support litigation.

Demonstrating Cross-Subsidization. A further technical problem lies down this route, however. It is one thing to establish a legal process, and another and quite different thing to be able to use it effectively. In order to do so, it must be shown that cross-subsidization is actually occurring.

The OECD is pessimistic that cross-subsidization can be demonstrated satisfactorily. It comments that:

> Given the difficulties of obtaining reliable cost information, anti-competitive cross-subsidisation may only be reliably prevented through structural or regulatory measures such as privatisation (as in the Netherlands), liberalisation (i.e. elimination of the remaining reserved areas) or horizontal or vertical separation. Horizontal separation involves preventing the incumbent postal operator from providing competitive services such as express or parcel services. . . . Vertical separation would involve separating final delivery from the remaining segments of the postal business. (OECD 1999, 11)

The conclusion that the best way of eliminating cross-subsidization is to separate PPOs from the provision of competitive services (which, in context, presumably means services that can in principle be supplied under conditions of competition) is probably correct. The problem, however, is that it would be unwise to anticipate agreement on such a step in the context of the GATS. The likely effectiveness of less radical steps is therefore important. If there were no effective means of showing cross-subsidization, the liberalizing process would be awkwardly poised between the status quo and radical reform, and the odds are that the status quo would prevail.

But the OECD is too pessimistic. In the first place, accounting data are not the only means of identifying cross-subsidization. An alternative means is comparison of prices and profits across PPOs. Suppose that the PPO of country A charges prices in its areas of exclusivity that are twice as high as those of country B's PPO, which is similar in all relevant respects. Suppose further that the former fails to make profits, while the latter succeeds. And suppose finally that the PPO in country A operates an express-delivery service for which it charges a very low price. With or without accounting data, these facts surely establish a prima facie case for cross-subsidization by country A's PPO.

Moreover, it is open to WTO members to decide that absolute proof of cross-subsidization is not necessary for legal consequences to flow. Given the difficulty of obtaining hard evidence, for example, establishment of a prima facie case might be deemed sufficient to shift the burden of proof. Thus, a prima facie case having been established, the PPO, to escape the legal consequences of engaging in cross-subsidization, would have to prove that it did not engage in such practices (and would probably want to call upon internal accounting data in its attempt to do so).

Conclusion on Facilitating Express Delivery

A number of problems beset international express delivery. In the organizational terms of the GATS, these problems could, in principle, be handled in several ways. They could be dealt with by an agreement on postal and express-delivery services, by a broader agreement on networks, or by inclusion in separate agreements— for example, on customs facilitation; NTBs in services trade; and the behavior of dominant suppliers.

The organizational structure, however, is less important than the effect. The GATS should deal with the problems facing providers of express-delivery service, and it should be capable of dealing with them.

6

Conclusion

If members of the international air transport industry were asked to choose between a TCAA and the entry of their industry into the GATS, it is a fair bet that a large majority would vote for a TCAA. Were negotiations on a TCAA to take place in the next five years, they would most likely be outside the GATS. As explained in chapter 4, however, a TCAA is not incompatible with the GATS. Indeed, a TCAA negotiated outside the GATS, but whose principal provisions are consistent with the GATS, may be the best way of eventually bringing international air transport and the GATS together.

Be that as it may, the prospects for bringing the core issue of international traffic rights into the GATS in the course of a revived Doha Round are small. That reflects in part protectionism in the industry.

But that is not the whole story. The air transport industry has been organized to provide services internationally for many years. It is a large and complex industry with its own intergovernmental treaties and organizations. Even in the most propitious circumstances, it would be unreasonable to expect the members of such an industry blithely to abandon its established practices and procedures to embrace new ones that are not specific to aviation and still in the course of development.

While not much is to be expected from Doha on traffic rights, however, there is considerable scope for expanding the list of services that are not "directly related to the exercise of traffic rights." There is also scope for action on air freight, if the definitional problems noted in chapter 5 can be overcome. That would be a valuable extension of the GATS, providing, so to speak, a dress rehearsal for the edification of the rest of the industry.

Undoubtedly, however, the greatest hopes for the outcome of the Doha Round as far as aviation or aviation-intensive industries are concerned lie with express delivery. The problems that surround the issue of applying the GATS to the air transport industry may block one route to the liberalization of the conditions facing express delivery. Another option is available, though. It is to negotiate agreements that deal with, or encompass, the difficulties facing express delivery—on customs procedures, nontariff barriers to delivery of the service, and the issues raised by competition with public postal operators.

Supporters of the GATS should enthusiastically press for that route to be followed. The object is valuable in itself. Moreover, if it can effectively deal with such issues, the GATS will establish its credentials to tackle larger ones—such as the eventual absorption of international air transport services into its structures.

Appendix
Largest Carriers and Alliances

Largest Carriers

Lists of the world's largest carriers vary dramatically with different measures of size. One crucial matter is that U.S. carriers have a higher proportion of domestic traffic than carriers elsewhere. Thus, ranked by passengers carried on all routes—domestic or international—the top five carriers in 2001 were all from the United States (Delta, United, American, U.S. Airways, and Northwest). Ranked by passengers carried on international routes, however, as shown in table 1, only one U.S. carrier appears in the top ten.

"International," though, includes flights between Frankfurt and Brussels. European carriers do more such short-hop international flights than U.S. carriers, so the average distance a passenger is carried varies sharply among carriers. Use of passenger-kilometers flown as the measure of size therefore changes the ranking. SAS (25), Air Canada (11), and Alitalia (20) exit the top ten, while United (4), Northwest (9), and Qantas (10) enter it.

The same phenomena manifest themselves when carriers are ranked by tonnes of freight carried. That measure, however, also introduces carriers whose principal business is freight. Table 2 gives the ten largest carriers on this measure.

Again, however, conversion to tonne-kilometers changes the ranking. EAT (38) and UPS (11) then exit the ranking. KLM (8) and Cargolux (10) enter it.

Table 1: Ten Largest Carriers, Ordered by Passengers Carried on International Routes, 2001

Carrier	Passengers (thousands)
Lufthansa	29,102
British Airways	28,113
Air France	24,379
American Airlines	16,264
KLM	15,783
Singapore Airlines	14,696
SAS	13,060
Japan Airlines	12,248
Air Canada	11,876
Alitalia	11,386

Source: IATA 2002, 48.

Table 2: Ten Largest Carriers, Ordered by Freight Tonnes Carried on International Routes, 2001

Carrier	Freight Tonnes Carried
Federal Express	1,295
Lufthansa	1,012
Singapore Airlines	930
Korean Airlines	892
United Parcel Service	729
Cathay Pacific	704
Air France	638
British Airways	593
Japan Airlines	567
EAT	549

Source: IATA 2002, 49.

Alliances

As noted in the text, alliances have become a major means of circumventing restrictions on commercial opportunity. There are four major alliances. The largest on almost all measures is Star (Air Canada, Air New Zealand, All Nippon Airlines, Austrian Airlines, bmi british midland, Lufthansa, Mexicana Airlines, SAS, Singapore Airlines, Thai, United Airlines, and Varig). The others are oneworld (Aer Lingus, American Airlines, British Airways, Cathay Pacific, Finnair, Iberia, LAN-Chile, and Qantas); Sky Team (Aeromexico, Air France, Alitalia, Czech Airlines, Delta Airlines, and Korea Airlines); and KLM/NW (KLM and Northwest Airlines). Table 3 gives the size of the alliances in terms of international passenger-kilometers.

Table 3: Passenger-Kilometers Flown by Major Alliances, 2001

Alliance	Passenger-Kilometers (millions)	Market Share (%)
Star	412,894	25
oneworld	309,531	19
Sky Team	198,221	12
KLM/NW	110,109	7

Source: IATA 2002, 47.

Notes

1. The texts of the Uruguay Round Agreements may be found in WTO (1995). The GATS may be found at WTO (1995), *Annex 1B*, 283–317.

2. One form of WTO agreement—a plurilateral agreement—applies to the subset of WTO members that accepts it, but not to the rest. In principle, therefore, it might be possible to construct a TCAA-type agreement in the WTO. Plurilateral agreements are discussed in chapter 4.

3. A government can, in principle, apply conditions to cabotage. Thus, for example, it could require that foreign carriers observe its safety regulations, or that they conform to the wage structures negotiated by the domestic industry. It seems simpler, for expositional purposes, to discuss cabotage in its basic form, without add-on conditions.

4. Civil Reserve Air Fleet website, available at http://www.af.mil/fact sheets/factsheet.asp?fsID=173, accessed January 6, 2004.

5. U.S.-based foreign-owned carriers probably would complain that they were discriminated against and their U.S.-owned competitors given state aid. It is difficult to believe, though, that non-U.S. carriers would reject a right of establishment in the United States on the ground that they were not admitted to membership of the Civil Reserve Air Fleet.

6. Airport economics is not straightforward. Fuller expositions than those given in this chapter may be found in U.S. Department of Transportation (1995) and Productivity Commission (2002), an Australian report.

7. The route offered by the *Annex* is still open, however, for maritime transport. Annexes to the GATS provided for post-Marrakesh negotiations in financial services, basic telecommunications, and maritime transport, and allowed the listing of MFN exemptions in those sectors to be postponed until the end of the negotiations. The negotiations on maritime transport were abandoned, still incomplete, in 1996. A *Decision on*

Maritime Transport Services, adopted by the Council for Trade in Services on June 28, 1996, said that negotiations would be resumed "with the commencement of comprehensive negotiations on services" and were to be concluded "no later than at the end of this first round of progressive liberalisation." The end of the negotiation on maritime transport therefore has not yet arrived, and the possibility of Article II exemptions in that sector survives. Paragraph 2 of the *Annex* provides an alternative but much harder route to MFN exemptions.

8. The wording of the *Annex on Air Transport Services* suggests that there are other "services directly related to the exercise of traffic rights," but it does not specify what these are and gives no indication of what services are to be regarded as not directly related to the exercise of traffic rights. Arguably, the category of such unrelated ancillary services is large. The provision of in-flight meals, for example, does not seem to have any intrinsic effect on traffic rights. It might therefore be argued that the GATS applies to that ancillary service, and perhaps to many others as well.

9. Nonviolation complaints have a potential role in aviation services, should the sector enter the GATS. In principle, nonviolation complaints could be used to address problems arising from subsidies and the application (or nonapplication) of competition law.

10. The imposition of sanctions in aviation disputes in the period between the failure of prescribed negotiations and the rendering of a decision in the arbitration—a right the United States claims in aviation disputes—would, however, be unusual under current WTO practice. It is not necessarily impossible, though. Article XXIII(2) of the GATS says: "If the DSB considers that the circumstances are serious enough . . . it may authorise a member or members to suspend the application . . . of obligations and specific commitments" (WTO 1995, 301).

11. A current example of this difficulty is provided by the prolonged negotiations between the governments of the United States and the UK to replace the Bermuda 2 agreement. U.S. providers of express-delivery services want fifth-freedom rights—that is, the right to pick up cargo and transport it to third countries—at Stanstead, one of London's airports. But detaching this request from the wider issues of, among others, access of U.S. passenger carriers to Heathrow and U.S. laws on foreign ownership of U.S. airlines, has not so far proved possible.

12. In February 1997, sixty-nine countries, accounting for more than 95 percent of world telecom revenues, agreed to major liberalization of trade in basic and value-added telecommunications services.

13. Sweden, Finland, and New Zealand have fully liberalized the provision of postal services and currently have no PPO with a monopoly in any class of mail.

14. "A few countries have completely liberalised their postal sector and other countries reserve a relatively small reserved area. The liberalising countries reported quality of service improvements, increases in profitability, increases in employment and real reductions in prices" (OECD 1999, 10).

15. Despite its great importance, the *Reference Paper* is difficult to reference. Formally, it is Appendix 3 to the Fourth Protocol to the GATS. The Fourth Protocol is an agreement on basic telecoms that postdated the Uruguay Round. The agreement was accepted, in whole or in part, by fifty-seven countries, and came into effect on February 5, 1998. However, it appears never to have been officially published by the WTO—hence the APEC reference above. A possible explanation—though not a satisfactory one—for its lack of official WTO publication is that countries could pick and choose among its provisions. There is therefore no single text that applies to all signatories.

References

Asia-Pacific Economic Cooperation (APEC). 1997. *Reference Paper to the Fourth Protocol to the GATS.* Available at http://www.apectel27.org.my/WTO/WTO-04.rtf.

Brooks, Rick. 2000. UPS Sues Canadian Government. *Wall Street Journal Europe,* April 25.

Done, Kevin. 2002. Light Shed on the Black Art of a Grey Market. *Financial Times,* July 12.

European Community. 1998. Directive 97/67/EU of December 15, 1997. In *Official Journal* L15/14. January 21.

Hindley, Brian. 1989. Integrated World Markets in Services: Problems and Prospects. In *Services in World Economic Growth,* ed. Herbert Giersch. Tubingen: J.C.B. Mohr [Paul Siebeck].

International Air Transport Association (IATA). 2002. *World Air Transport Statistics.* IATA Aviation Information and Research Department. Montreal, June.

Mattoo, Aaditya. 1997. *Dealing with Monopolies and State Enterprises: WTO Rules for Goods and Services.* Unpublished manuscript.

Moore, Mike. 2002. Aviation Industry Must Stop Flying Solo. *Times* (London), August 2, 27.

Organisation for Economic Co-operation and Development (OECD). Secretariat. 1999. *Promoting Competition in Postal Services.* DAFFE/CLP (99)22. October 1.

Productivity Commission. 2002. *Price Regulation of Airport Services.* Inquiry Report No. 19. Canberra, January 23.

Reyna, Jimmy. 1998. *Comments before the Trade Policy Staff Committee, Office of the United States Trade Representative, on behalf of the US ExITS Sector regarding initial U.S. negotiating objectives for the nine negotiating groups of the Free Trade Area of the Americas.* Washington, D.C., July 29.

U.S. Department of Transportation. 1995. *Report to the Congress: A Study of the High Density Rule.* Washington, D.C., May.

World Trade Organization (WTO). 1995. *WTO Legal Texts: The Uruguay Round Agreements.* Available at http://www.wto.org/english/docs_e/legal_e/legal_e.htm. Accessed January 6, 2004. Also available in World Trade Organization (WTO). 1995. *The Legal Texts: the Results of the Uruguay Round of Multilateral Trade Negotiations.* Cambridge, England: Cambridge University Press.

———. 1998. *Air Transport Services.* S/C/W/59. November 5.

About the Author

Brian Hindley is Emeritus Reader in Trade Policy Economics at the London School of Economics. He is a consultant on trade policy to a number of international organizations and businesses, including the European Commission, the World Bank, and the Organisation for Economic Co-operation and Development. Mr. Hindley received his AB and PhD from the University of Chicago.